Author – Robert J

Published by Robert J Promotions

ISBN 9781068218866

ISBN 978-1-0682188-6-6

9 781068 218866 >

Title Page

100 Wealth Manifestations

Robert J

About The Author

Robert J

Robert J is a dedicated researcher and writer who believes that every problem has already been solved—the key is finding the right answer. With a sharp eye for overlooked truths and a passion for uncovering practical solutions, he brings forward time-tested wisdom to help readers navigate financial and life challenges and life's biggest decisions. His work is not about reinventing the wheel—it's about revealing the proven strategies that empower people to break free from limitations and build lasting success. Through meticulous research and clear, actionable insights, Robert J transforms complex ideas into powerful lessons, accessible to all. His mission is simple: to bridge the gap between knowledge and action, so readers can take control of their future with confidence.

In particular with concerns about today's economics Robert J is aware of the struggles so many people are having just trying to make ends meet. The biggest issue is that money as a concept is not taught in schools and few families understand it properly.

There is absolutely no reason why everyone should not learn about money and how to create wealth in their own lives. It's just a matter of education and action. Even the great Elon Musk started out poor but put in the effort to learn about finance, money and how to "work the system" legally.

You may not displace Elon as the richest person but you can transform your own life and that of your family.

That's why the author has created a whole series of short, action packed books aimed at people in all walks of life. Surprisingly nearly everyone develops skills and talents in their everyday lives that could be used to improve their wealth situation if they just knew how.

Such books are: “Wealth For Housewives”, “Wealth For Teachers”, “Wealth For Engineers”, etc. and more are being written all the time.

Use the QR code below to sign up to the author's mailing list. From time to time you will get an email with details of new publications that could help you transform your life.

CHAPTERS

1. The Energetics of Wealth: Why Manifestation Works
A breakdown of how thought patterns, emotional frequencies, and subconscious beliefs influence financial outcomes—and why wealth isn't just strategy, it's energy.

2. Busting Manifestation Myths
Clarifies misconceptions like "just visualize and money appears," and replaces them with grounded, action-based mindset shifts. Perfect for readers skeptical or burned by spiritual clichés.

3. The Subconscious Wallet: Rewiring Your Inner Beliefs About Money
How childhood scripts, societal programming, and scarcity conditioning silently block wealth—and how manifestation rewrites those beliefs.

4. The Aligned Manifestor's Toolkit
Key tools readers can integrate: visualization, scripting, gratitude journaling, wealth mantras, emotional regulation, and intentional action.

5. Manifestation and Financial Discipline: Partners, Not Opposites
Blending intuitive practices with budgeting, investing, and strategy—how manifestation doesn't replace discipline, it *amplifies* it.

6. The 5 Laws of Wealth Manifestation
A chapter detailing core principles like: clarity of vision, emotional alignment, action congruence, energetic neutrality, and delayed reward orientation.

7. Daily Rituals to Prime Your Mind for Wealth
Morning and evening habits to raise financial self-worth and stay magnetized toward abundance: affirmations, breathwork, visualization, micro-journaling.

8. From Wishful to Wealthy: Building a Manifestation Habit That Sticks
Addresses how to make manifestation more than a fleeting trend—embedding it as a lifestyle practice that compounds over time.

9. The Role of Patience, Timing, and Trust in Abundance
A mindset-shifting chapter for those discouraged by delays; reframing divine timing and energetic preparation.

10. Your Wealth Identity: Becoming the Version of You Who Has It All
The psychology of self-concept and its magnetic pull—teaching readers to act, think, and receive as if they already are abundant.

11: Wealth Boundaries – Protecting the Flow You've Created

Wealth boundaries are the energetic, emotional, and financial safeguards that preserve your abundance, ensuring your flow stays aligned, protected, and empowered.

12: Unlocking the Twelfth Gate

Unlocking the Twelfth Gate" reveals that true wealth is not something to attain, but a state of being to embody—where abundance flows from within as a natural expression of your highest self.

Chapter 1: *The Energetics of Wealth: Why Manifestation Works*

Most people think wealth is built through strategy, hustle, and spreadsheets. While action is vital, what often gets ignored is the undercurrent shaping those actions—the silent architecture of our thoughts, emotions, and energy. Manifestation isn't just magic thinking. It's mindset engineering. And in this chapter, we explore why true wealth begins far before the first pound is earned.

The Frequency of Thought

Every thought carries an energetic signature. Neuroscience shows us that repetitive thought patterns form neural pathways that condition our perception of reality. When we continually tell ourselves, *"I'll never be good with money"* or *"I'm just not a numbers person,"* we unconsciously prime our brains to seek confirmation of these beliefs.

But the reverse is also true. With intentionality, new narratives create new neurological patterns—ones that support wealth attraction, not resistance. This is the first energetic layer of financial manifestation: *reprogramming your inner script.*

Emotional Currency: The Power of Feeling

Emotions are amplifiers. A passing thought with no emotional weight fades quickly. But a thought charged with fear, shame, or joy has staying power. If you carry anxiety around money, that emotion *colors your decisions*: you might avoid looking at your bank account, undercharge for your services, or self-sabotage investments.

To manifest from an empowered space, it's not enough to *think* positively—you must *feel* it. Practicing emotional congruence, like gratitude, abundance, and certainty, helps align your inner environment with the financial outcomes you desire.

Subconscious Blocks: The Unseen Saboteur

Our beliefs about money are often formed in childhood—passed down through family narratives like *"money doesn't grow on trees"* or *"rich people are greedy."* These subconscious scripts operate in the background, quietly dictating our relationship with wealth.

To shift these, you must become aware of them. Journaling, affirmations, and inner child work are powerful tools for identifying and rewriting the "invisible contracts" you've inherited. Only when these blocks are dissolved can your conscious goals truly take root.

Aligning Action with Energy

Manifestation without action is wishful thinking. But action without energetic alignment is exhausting. True wealth-building harmonizes both. This means taking aligned steps—whether that's opening an investment account, raising your rates, or applying for a new role—while staying rooted in the belief that you *deserve* and *can sustain* financial abundance.

It's about acting from faith, not fear. About taking practical steps *as if* the outcome is inevitable—because energetically, it already is.

Closing Reflection: You Are the Signal

Wealth isn't something you chase. It's something you *tune into*. When your thoughts, emotions, and subconscious beliefs are in harmony, you broadcast a signal—energetic clarity—that the world responds to. Clients find you. Opportunities emerge. Finances shift.

Not because the universe randomly decides to bless you, but because *you've become the type of person it naturally flows to.*

✍ Guided Journaling: *Activating Your Wealth Frequency*

Set aside 10–15 minutes. Find a quiet space. Breathe deeply. Then respond to the prompts below with honesty and compassion. The goal isn't perfection—it's *pattern awareness and energetic recalibration.*

1. Early Imprints
What's your first memory of money? How did it feel—safe, scarce, joyful, stressful?
How might this memory still be shaping your beliefs today?

2. Emotional Currency Check-In
When I think about money right now, I feel _______.
Where do I feel that in my body? Is there tension, ease, pressure, warmth?

3. Rewrite the Script
What is a money belief I've inherited that I no longer want to carry?
What new belief do I choose to replace it with?

4. Energetic Alignment Snapshot
What thoughts, emotions, or actions in my current financial life *support* abundance?

What thoughts or behaviors feel out of alignment with the version of me who's financially free?

5. Future Frequency
If I were already living my wealthiest life, how would I walk into a room?
What would I say yes to? What would I release?

Wealth Energy Affirmations

These aren't just mantras—they're *neurological directives*. Speak them aloud, write them down, or record them in your voice and listen daily. Use them to recalibrate your emotional and energetic relationship with money.

- I am a powerful creator, and wealth flows naturally to me.
- My energy is aligned with prosperity, peace, and purpose.
- It is safe for me to receive more than enough.
- I rewire old beliefs and claim my financial freedom.
- Abundance responds to who I am—not just what I do.
- I am becoming the version of me who magnetizes aligned wealth with ease.
- My financial reality is a reflection of my healed inner world—and I am healing beautifully.

Chapter 2: *Busting Manifestation Myths*

You've seen the headlines. *"Visualize wealth and it'll appear!"* or *"The Universe is your ATM."* At first glance, manifestation sounds like a cosmic vending machine: think rich, get rich. But behind the glitter of these catchphrases lies a deeper truth—one that requires more than daydreams and mood boards.

If you've ever rolled your eyes at the idea of "manifesting money," you're not alone. This chapter is here to cut through the fluff, expose the myths, and replace them with grounded, action-based mindset shifts that *actually* create results.

Myth 1: *"Just Visualize It and the Money Will Appear"*

Visualization is a tool, not a guarantee. Yes, elite athletes, performers, and entrepreneurs use mental rehearsal to improve performance. But they also *train*, *show up*, and *do the work.*

Think of visualization as mental priming—it sets the brain's GPS. But you still have to fuel the car, press the pedal, and steer through traffic. Without aligned action, visualizing a million pounds is just a fancy nap.

> **Mindset Shift:** Use vision to clarify your goals, then reverse-engineer them into action steps. Align imagination with intention.

Myth 2: *"High Vibes Only!"*

The law of attraction is often boiled down to staying happy 24/7. But humans aren't built for emotional flatlining. Avoiding negative feelings doesn't raise your vibration—it represses your humanity.

In fact, financial growth *requires* processing uncomfortable emotions like guilt, shame, and fear. They're signals—not failures. Denying them keeps you stuck; working with them sets you free.

> **Mindset Shift:** Emotional fluency is key. Instead of suppressing discomfort, ask, *"What's this feeling trying to teach me about my financial beliefs?"*

Myth 3: *"If It's Not Happening, You're Not Aligned"*

Spiritual circles often suggest that if your goals aren't manifesting, *you're the problem*. That's toxic. Sometimes things don't happen because they take time. Or because you're learning critical lessons in the meantime. Or because external systems (hello, wealth inequality) create real barriers.

> **Mindset Shift:** Alignment isn't about perfection. It's about *resilience*. Stay curious, not self-critical. Progress is still progress, even if it looks messy.

Myth 4: *"Money Is Just Energy"*

Yes, money carries energetic charge. But it's also legal tender. Bills still need paying. Investments still require due diligence. Clients still expect delivery.

While energy influences flow, money *exists within systems*. Ignoring strategy in favor of "vibes only" keeps people in cycles of wishful thinking, not wealth creation.

> **Mindset Shift:** Pair energy with education. Learn to manage money as both a mindset *and* a skill set.

Myth 5: *"Detach Completely and It Will Come"*

Detachment is often misunderstood as indifference. But letting go isn't giving up—it's releasing *obsession*. True detachment means *trusting* that your actions will yield results, even if they don't unfold on your timeline.

> **Mindset Shift:** Practice *committed detachment*: Stay engaged with your goals, while allowing outcomes to evolve organically.

Closing Reflection: The Empowered Skeptic

Skepticism isn't the enemy of manifestation—it's the ally of discernment. When you cut through the noise, you become Empowered, Grounded, Intentional.

Manifestation doesn't replace hard work—it *redirects* it. Instead of chasing money from a place of fear or lack, you show up with clarity, confidence, and conscious action. That's where real transformation happens.

Bonus Page: *Truth vs Myth — The Manifestation Clarifier*

Myth	Truth
"Manifestation is just wishful thinking."	Manifestation is focused intention, aligned action, and belief working together —not magic, but mindset.
"If it doesn't happen fast, it means I'm doing it wrong."	Timing isn't always instant. Delayed results often reflect the

Myth	Truth
	unfolding of your readiness and the universe's rhythm.
"You must be positive 24/7 for manifestation to work."	Authenticity > toxic positivity. Acknowledge doubts, then choose belief anyway—that's real power.
"Money isn't spiritual—manifesting wealth is greedy."	Wealth is a tool. When used with purpose, it enables generosity, creativity, and freedom—deeply spiritual outcomes.
"Visualization alone is enough."	Visualization primes your subconscious, but it needs your aligned action to ground it in reality.

Reflection Worksheet: Rewriting the Inner Script

Part 1: Identifying Hidden Myths

List any money or manifestation beliefs you've held that might be quietly sabotaging your progress.

1.
2.
3.

Part 2: What's Actually True for Me?

Choose one belief and rewrite it as a powerful truth:

Old belief: ______________________________

New truth: ________________________________

Part 3: Breakthrough Prompts

1. *When I think about wealth, what emotions come up—and are they mine or inherited?*
2. *What proof do I have that I can manifest meaningful change in my life?*
3. *What's one small action I can take this week to back up my manifestation with momentum?*

Chapter 3: *The Subconscious Wallet: Rewiring Your Inner Beliefs About Money*

Before you ever earned your first paycheck, you'd already formed a relationship with money. Not consciously—but deep in the fabric of your subconscious. It's the emotional wallet you carry into every financial decision. And if it's stuffed with fear, guilt, or scarcity, no amount of budgeting or investing can fully override its influence.

To manifest money differently, you must *believe* differently. Let's unpack the unseen scripts running the show—and how to change them.

Inheritance You Didn't Ask For: Childhood Money Scripts

You might not remember the first time you overheard "We can't afford that" or "Money is the root of all evil"—but your nervous system does. Childhood is where our primary money blueprint is shaped. Whether you grew up in struggle, survival, or excess, emotional imprints were formed.

Some examples:

- *If love was withheld around money*, you may now equate wealth with unworthiness.
- *If money caused stress*, you may associate having it with anxiety.
- *If success was frowned upon*, you may dim your ambition out of loyalty or guilt.

Key Insight: These early beliefs become your *default financial setting*, quietly dictating how much you allow yourself to earn, keep, or enjoy. Families should be nuturing and enabling. But sometimes the reverse is true.

Culture & Conditioning: Society's Scarcity Spell

Beyond family, you've been conditioned by media, advertising, religion, and systemic structures. You've likely absorbed beliefs like:

- "Making money requires sacrificing your soul."
- "It's selfish to want more."
- "If I succeed, someone else has to lose."

These ideas frame money as either morally corrupt or perilously scarce. No wonder so many people feel conflicted about their desire for abundance—it's been framed as both noble to reject and shameful to pursue.

> **Reframe:** Money doesn't corrupt character—it *amplifies* it. Generous people with money fund movements, support communities, and change lives.

The Subconscious Wallet in Action

Unconscious beliefs surface in subtle ways:

- Underpricing your services
- Avoiding your bank statements
- Procrastinating on applying for a raise
- Feeling guilty after a financial win

These aren't random behaviors. They're protective mechanisms—your subconscious trying to maintain safety and familiarity, even if it sabotages success.

Rewriting the Script: How Manifestation Recodes the Mind

True manifestation starts with awareness. You can't change what you don't acknowledge. Here's how to rewire:

1. **Identify the Script:** Journal your memories around money. Whose voice do you hear? What phrases repeat in your mind?
2. **Challenge the Belief:** Is it absolutely true that "money changes people"? Or is it that it *reveals* them?
3. **Introduce New Truths:** Use affirmations that speak directly to your inner child. Example: *"It's safe for me to be wealthy and kind."*
4. **Create Micro-Proof:** Take small actions that contradict your old belief—like raising your prices or opening a savings account just for joy.

Remember: The subconscious learns through repetition and emotion. Marry your new beliefs with feeling, and practice them like a daily ritual.

Closing Reflection: Your Mind is the Vault

You are not your past. You are the author of your financial future. Every time you choose to examine a limiting belief and rewrite it, you *upgrade your wallet from the inside out.*

The wealth you want isn't just in your strategy—it's in your story. And you get to tell a new one, starting now.

Money-Limiting Belief Quiz: What's Blocking Your Abundance?

Tick the statements that resonate with you, even a little:

- [ ] I feel guilty or selfish wanting more money.
- [ ] I believe I have to work extremely hard to earn a decent living.
- [ ] I avoid checking my bank account—it makes me anxious.
- [ ] Wealthy people are often greedy or dishonest.
- [ ] There's never enough money to go around.
- [ ] I'm just not good with money.
- [ ] Talking about money makes me uncomfortable.
- [ ] I often sabotage myself when things start going well financially.
- [ ] It feels safer to expect less than risk being disappointed.
- [ ] I fear judgment if I become "too" successful.

Score Interpretation:

- **0–2**: Your subconscious wallet is ready to be filled—keep reinforcing what's working.
- **3–6**: You're carrying beliefs that might be limiting your potential—time for a mindset tune-up.
- **7–10**: Money wounds are calling for deep healing—this chapter is your invitation to start.

Wealth Rewrite Journaling Prompts

Prompt 1: The Origin Story
Where did your earliest ideas about money come from? What messages did you receive at home, in school, or in your community?

Prompt 2: The Reframe
Choose one money-limiting belief you've identified. Write a new story—what empowering truth do you want to believe instead?

Prompt 3: The Future Self Letter

Write a letter from your future self who is financially confident, calm, and creative. What do they want you to know right now?

Prompt 4: The Bold Action Anchor
What's one bold, belief-shifting action you can take this week that aligns with your new money identity?

Chapter 4: *The Aligned Manifestor's Toolkit*

Creating wealth from alignment isn't passive—it's intentional. Just like an athlete trains their body, aligned manifestors train their mind, nervous system, and energetic presence. Not once, not occasionally, but *consistently.* This chapter equips readers with practical, repeatable tools to turn manifestation from concept into lived practice.

These aren't fluffy rituals. They're *neuroscientific, somatic, and strategic exercises* designed to shift identity, embody belief, and prompt bold action. Choose the ones that resonate now—and return to the rest when ready. Each tool is a key. Together, they open the vault.

1. Visualization: See It to Believe It

When you vividly imagine your future success, you activate the same neural circuitry as if it were already happening. Your body doesn't know the difference between reality and mental rehearsal —it simply responds.

> ✅ *Do this:* Close your eyes for 3 minutes each morning and *visualize your wealth goals already accomplished.* Feel the gratitude. See the email confirming the deal. Hear yourself saying, "I did it." Anchor it in your senses.
>
> *Pro Tip:* Add physicality—smile, stand taller, breathe deeper. Make it visceral.

2. Scripting: Be the Author of Your Future

Scripting is journaling as if your ideal financial life has already happened. It's not fiction—it's direction. Writing in the present tense imprints the subconscious with clarity and confidence.

> ✍ *Prompt:* "I'm so grateful now that I've hit my 5-figure month. The clients are soul-aligned, the work flows with ease, and I've never felt so energized."
>
> Do this daily or weekly. Repetition + emotion = new subconscious groove.

3. Gratitude Journaling: Expand What You Appreciate

Gratitude is a frequency match for abundance. When you consciously recognize what *is* going well, you signal to your brain, *"This is important—find more of it."* It cultivates receiving energy, which is essential for wealth attraction.

> *Prompt:* "Today I'm grateful for…"

- The $10 refund that arrived out of the blue
- The compliment that reminded me I'm on track
- The peace I felt while budgeting

> *Shift from scarcity to overflow* by training your attention to see what's already abundant.

4. Wealth Mantras: Speak Your Identity into Reality

Words shape beliefs. Repeating money mantras isn't about tricking yourself—it's about building neural repetition around empowering truths.

Examples:

- "I trust myself with money."
- "I attract aligned wealth with ease."
- "My income expands as I do."

Say them aloud. Say them in the mirror. Say them when you don't feel ready—that's when they work best.

5. Emotional Regulation: Create Inner Safety for Outer Expansion

Manifestation gets blocked not by lack of desire, but by lack of emotional safety. The nervous system must *feel safe* to receive more. If abundance triggers fear, guilt, or imposter syndrome, those emotions can sabotage even the best plans.

> *Practice:* Box breathing, EFT tapping, or somatic shaking to discharge fear.

These practices are like energetic reset buttons for the nervous system. Here's how to do these exercises:

The Aligned Manifestor's Toolkit: Discharging Fear Through the Body

1. Box Breathing (a.k.a. Four-Square Breathing)
This Navy SEAL-approved technique calms the fight-or-flight response and brings the body into a state of grounded focus.

How to Practice:

- Inhale through your nose for 4 seconds
- Hold your breath for 4 seconds

- Exhale slowly through your mouth for 4 seconds
- Hold again for 4 seconds
  Repeat for 4–6 rounds.
  Use this before journaling, visualizing, or making financial decisions to anchor your energy.

2. EFT Tapping (Emotional Freedom Technique)
Tapping on acupressure points while acknowledging fear helps rewire emotional patterns and restore balance.

How to Practice:

- Identify a fear or limiting belief (e.g., "I'm afraid I'll never have enough money")
- Rate the intensity (1–10)
- Tap gently on these points while repeating a setup phrase:
    - *Side of hand (karate chop point)*: "Even though I feel this fear, I deeply and completely accept myself."
    - *Eyebrow, side of eye, under eye, under nose, chin, collarbone, under arm, top of head*—tap each point while repeating a shortened version like "this fear"
- After a few rounds, re-rate the intensity and notice any shifts.
  This is especially powerful when paired with your affirmations from earlier chapters.

3. Somatic Shaking
This primal, instinctive movement helps discharge stored tension and trauma from the body—like hitting reset on your nervous system.

How to Practice:

- Stand with feet hip-width apart
- Begin to gently bounce your knees and let your arms hang loose

- Allow your body to shake naturally—start small and let it build
- Shake for 1–3 minutes, then pause and feel the sensations
- Finish with a deep breath and a grounding touch (e.g., hand on heart or belly)
  Use this when fear feels stuck in your body or after a stressful event.

These tools don't just soothe—they *reclaim* your power.

Fear Release Flow: A 5-Minute Ritual to Reset and Realign

Use this flow whenever fear feels louder than your vision. It's designed to help you *return to center*, release stored tension, and realign with your power.

Step 1: Box Breathing (1 minute)
Calm your nervous system and anchor your presence.
➤ *Inhale for 4... Hold 4... Exhale 4... Hold 4...* (Repeat 4–6 rounds)
With each breath, imagine fear loosening its grip.

Step 2: EFT Tapping (2 minutes)
Gently tap through the points while saying:
"Even though I feel afraid, I choose to trust myself and this journey."
Continue tapping while naming the fear, e.g., *"Fear of failing... Fear of not being enough..."*
Notice the shift in your emotional intensity—release comes with awareness, not resistance.

Step 3: Somatic Shaking (1–2 minutes)
Stand up, bounce gently, and let your body shake off the lingering tension.
➤ Let it get messy, wild, intuitive.

This is your nervous system saying: "We're safe now."

Step 4: Ground and Affirm
Place your hand on your heart or belly. Speak this aloud or write it down:
"I release fear. I realign with belief. My body, my breath, and my mind are safe to move forward."
Let this be your permission slip to keep manifesting boldly.

Train your body to associate financial growth with safety, not threat. This is repeated to reinforce that the actions need repitition to be effective.

6. Intentional Action: Walk It Like You Talk It

The Universe meets you halfway—but you have to show up for your half. Inspired action is action taken from belief, not desperation. It bridges imagination with embodiment.

> Ask daily: "What's one action I can take that reflects my belief in wealth today?" — Send the pitch. Raise the rate. Invest in the skill. Follow the nudge.
>
> When your actions match your identity, results follow. Not instantly—but *inevitably.*

Closing Reflection: Integration Over Perfection

This isn't about doing *everything perfectly.* It's about *doing something consistently.* You're not building a shrine to money—you're building *resonance with prosperity.* One journal entry, one breath, one belief at a time.

Use these tools not as pressure, but as power. You are no longer just thinking about wealth. You are *training for it.*

Daily Alignment Tracker: Make Your Magic Measurable

Consistency is the amplifier of alignment. To help you embody your vision daily, use the **Daily Alignment Tracker**—a simple tool to keep you connected to your manifestation mindset, energy, and action.

✔ Did I ground my energy today? (Box breathing, EFT, or shaking)
✔ Did I speak or write an empowering affirmation?
✔ Did I take one aligned action toward my vision—no matter how small?
✔ Did I reframe a limiting belief that surfaced?
✔ Did I celebrate a win—internal or external?

Progress is the practice. Alignment isn't about perfection—it's about returning, again and again, to your power.

Additional Elements for the Daily Alignment Tracker

Mindset Pulse
Did I notice and shift one unhelpful thought pattern today?

Visualization Check-In
Did I spend at least 2 minutes visualizing my desired reality—how it *feels*, looks, and moves?

Intuitive Nudge
Did I listen to my inner guidance or take action based on a gut feeling?

Nervous System Score (1–5)
How regulated did I feel today?
➤ 1 = Overwhelmed / Freeze mode
➤ 5 = Calm, grounded, expansive

⚡ **Manifestor's Spark**
Did I do something today that made me feel powerful, creative, or magnetic?

Affirmation Anchor of the Day
Write the one affirmation you embodied most fully today.

Micro-Commitment Tracker
List one 5-minute or less action that aligned with your current money goals.

Recommitment Ritual
Did I consciously recommit to my vision, even if today was messy?

These elements make the tracker not only a record-keeping tool, but a *mirror* for alignment and emotional leadership.

Chapter 5: *Manifestation and Financial Discipline: Partners, Not Opposites*

There's a widespread myth in personal development that you must choose between flow and structure, intuition and spreadsheets, vision boards and balance sheets. But the truth is this: *Manifestation and discipline are not opposites—they're soulmates*. When blended with intention, your spiritual alignment becomes a strategy amplifier, not a substitute for it.

Wealth isn't just what you attract—it's what you *manage, build, and multiply*. And that requires both inner alignment and outer organization.

The False Binary: Magic vs. Math

Spiritual circles often preach detachment, surrender, and vibes. Financial circles push budgets, KPIs, and compound interest. But when you place these in opposition, you limit your power.

Think of manifestation as your *internal compass*—it gives you direction, clarity, and purpose. Financial discipline is the *vehicle*—it gets you where you're going, steadily and sustainably.

> Intuition without action = stuck.
> Discipline without vision = burnout.
> Together = financial sovereignty.

Manifestation Sets the Intention

The work begins inside:

- What do you *truly* want?
- Why does it matter?

- Who are you becoming in the process?

When you visualize a life of financial peace, or script yourself thriving, you activate your *reticular activating system*—a part of the brain that starts filtering in opportunities and ideas that match your vision.

This is why clarity is magnetic. But magnetism alone isn't the goal. What you attract must be honored through action.

Discipline Builds the Foundation

Here's where manifestation gets legs.

Budgeting:

Not restriction—*allocation*. You're telling your money where to go based on your values, not your fears.

Saving:

Evidence of *self-trust*. You're proving to yourself that you can delay gratification to receive even more later.

Investing:

Faith in motion. You're planting seeds for future abundance—and that's manifestation embodied.

Tracking:

Neutral data, not emotional drama. Awareness equals power. You can't improve what you won't look at.

> Financial discipline isn't anti-abundance. It's *evidence that you're preparing to steward more.*

Energetics in Practice: From Dreaming to Doing

Let's say you set a manifestation goal: "Earn £10,000 in 90 days."

Now pair it with discipline:

- **Daily visualization:** See yourself receiving with ease.
- **Strategic planning:** What offer, product, or service will generate that income?
- **Consistent execution:** Set marketing days, sales targets, and progress check-ins.
- **Emotional regulation:** Manage fear of rejection or visibility blocks as they arise.

This is manifestation in action. And *action is how belief becomes behavior.*

When One Is Missing…

- **Manifestation without discipline** feels scattered, inconsistent, and vague.
- **Discipline without manifestation** feels rigid, exhausting, and soulless.

Together, they build momentum with meaning. Structure with soul. Logic with magic.

Closing Reflection: You Are the Bridge

You are not too "woo" for strategy. You are not too "structured" for spirituality. You are the bridge between what's possible and what's planned.

Let your spreadsheets reflect your worth. Let your rituals reinforce your habits. Let your financial goals be both *soul-aligned and skill-executed.*

Because in the new paradigm of wealth—you don't choose

between vision and discipline. *You weave them into legacy.*

Action + Alignment: Where Dreams Meet Decisions

Manifestation isn't just vision boards and affirmations—it's follow-through with integrity. Use this check-in to harmonize your inner alignment with outer execution:

Inner Alignment

- Did I begin today with a clear intention or affirmation?
- Did I center myself before making financial choices?
- Did I act from belief, not fear?

Outer Action

- Did I make one disciplined financial decision today?
- Did I track or review my money flow without judgment?
- Did I honor a budget, savings, or investment commitment —even in a small way?

Discipline is devotion in motion. Every action taken from alignment becomes a signal to the universe—and a promise to yourself.

Chapter 6: *The 5 Laws of Wealth Manifestation*

Manifestation isn't just a vibe—it's a *structure for sustainable success*. Behind every aligned manifestation lies a system of principles quietly working in the background. These are not rigid commandments, but fluid laws—universal truths that, when understood and integrated, transform your relationship with wealth.

The most empowered manifestors don't just visualize abundance. They *live in alignment with these five laws*—day after day, decision after decision.

Let's break them down.

Law 1: Clarity of Vision

Vague intentions create vague outcomes. Without a clear vision of what you want—and why you want it—manifestation becomes a guessing game.

Clarity isn't just about numbers like "£5k a month." It's about *context*:

- Where are you earning from?
- Who are you helping?
- What does your wealthy life *look*, *feel*, and *flow* like?

Practice: Write out a 90-day wealth vision in vivid detail. Anchor it with sensory language and emotional resonance. Clarity breeds magnetism.

Law 2: Emotional Alignment

You don't attract what you *say* you want. You attract what you *feel safe* having.

If part of you believes wealth brings isolation, pressure, or guilt, you'll unconsciously repel it. Emotional alignment means that your nervous system, belief system, and emotional body are *in agreement* with your financial desires.

> **Practice:** Use breathwork, tapping, or somatic practices to soothe financial anxiety. Affirm: *"It's safe for me to receive and expand."*

Emotional congruence isn't about forcing positivity. It's about creating *inner permission* for outer prosperity.

Law 3: Action Congruence

The Universe responds not just to belief—but to *behavior.* You can't manifest a wealthy reality while acting like someone afraid to check their bank account.

Congruent action means your daily choices *match the identity of someone who already has the outcome.* It closes the gap between intention and embodiment.

> **Practice:** Ask yourself: *"What would future-me do today?"* Then do it. That becomes your calibration.

No action is too small when it reflects your future self.

Law 4: Energetic Neutrality

This is the most misunderstood law. Neutrality isn't apathy—it's detachment from desperate, anxious gripping. When you need money to show up *right now or else*, you introduce resistance.

Neutrality is *knowing it's on the way*, without obsessively checking the clock. It's desire without desperation.

> **Practice:** Reframe delays as alignment, not denial. Use the mantra: *"My desires are inevitable; my timeline is unfolding."*

When you release your emotional charge, you become a clearer channel for receiving.

Law 5: Delayed Reward Orientation

Instant gratification is the enemy of long-term wealth. Manifestation honors compound effort—done consistently, before visible results arrive.

This law teaches you to trust in *the lag*, not fear it. You become someone who sows diligently, waters patiently, and reaps wisely.

> **Practice:** Track behaviors, not just outcomes. Celebrate inputs like pitching, budgeting, or saving—before the money hits.

Wealth isn't just built in windfalls. It's built in *ritualized resilience.*

Closing Reflection: These Laws Are Already in You

You're not learning to become someone new. You're *remembering the version of you* who lives by these laws naturally: the clear, calm, consistent, courageous version.

Start with one law. Then layer the rest. Each one strengthens the other. And together, they transform you from someone who hopes to receive… into someone who *expects it, prepares for it, and fully inhabits it.*

Manifestation Alignment Audit: Are You Living the 5 Laws?

Use this self-check to reflect on how aligned your energy, mindset, and action are with the 5 Laws of Wealth Manifestation. Revisit weekly to spot patterns, growth, and opportunities to realign.

Law 1: Clarity of Vision
☐ Do I know *what* I want and *why* I want it?
☐ Have I clarified my next financial milestone or desire?

Law 2: Emotional Congruence
☐ Are my thoughts, emotions, and words aligned with abundance?
☐ Did I notice and shift any scarcity-based reactions this week?

Law 3: Embodied Action
☐ Did I take one bold action from belief, not fear?
☐ Am I balancing inspired flow with strategic follow-through?

Law 4: Receptivity & Trust
☐ Did I practice receiving—help, compliments, money, ideas?
☐ Where am I still trying to control outcomes rather than trust the process?

Law 5: Integration Over Time
☐ Am I staying committed when results aren't instant?
☐ How have I evolved emotionally or energetically since I began this journey?

Alignment isn't a final destination—it's a daily invitation.

Chapter 7: *Daily Rituals to Prime Your Mind for Wealth*

Manifestation isn't a one-time visualization—it's a *way of showing up every day*. Just as an athlete trains their body and a musician rehearses their craft, aligned manifestors train their *inner state* to become a match for financial abundance.

The key is consistency. Small practices—done with intention—build powerful neural and energetic patterns. This chapter offers a daily ritual blueprint designed to shift your identity, raise your self-worth, and magnetize wealth with calm certainty.

These are not just tasks—they're transformation on repeat.

The Power of Ritual

Why rituals work:

- They create *predictability for the nervous system*
- They anchor your energy before life's chaos kicks in
- They train your brain to *associate wealth with safety, gratitude, and readiness*

Your identity is built through repetition. These rituals reinforce the identity of someone who expects, prepares for, and *receives* abundance.

Morning Rituals: *Begin as the Wealthy You*

1. Affirmation Activation
Repeat empowering money mantras aloud. The goal is not perfection—it's *resonance*.

Examples:

- "I am a magnet for aligned wealth."
- "Abundance is my natural state."
- "I am safe, capable, and ready to receive."

Speak them standing tall, with breath and conviction. You're speaking *into identity.*

2. Breathwork for Expansion
Try a 3–5 minute *box breathing* pattern (inhale 4, hold 4, exhale 4, hold 4) or *breath of fire* for energizing your body. Breathwork clears stagnation and raises frequency.

> Wealth flows through openness. Clear your channels before you check your inbox.

3. Micro-Visualization
For 2–5 minutes, close your eyes and visualize your financial goals *as already done.* See yourself waking up in your dream home, reviewing your thriving finances, or celebrating a big win.

> Amplify this by smiling and feeling it in your body. The more real it feels, the more your brain believes it.

4. Future-Self Journaling
Use 3–5 bullet points to script as if today is already successful and abundant.

> ✍ Example:

- "I received unexpected income today."
- "My confidence was magnetic on that call."
- "I trusted myself fully with money."

This primes your subconscious to *seek matching evidence* all day.

Evening Rituals: *Close the Loop with Gratitude and Refinement*

1. Gratitude Scan

Before bed, write or speak three things you're grateful for related to money, value, or progress.

Examples:

- "I paid a bill with peace today."
- "I got a kind message from a past client."
- "I found £5 I forgot I had—proof of overflow."

Gratitude turns survival into abundance.

2. Wealth Reflection

Ask: *"How did I show up as my wealthy self today?"*
This reinforces identity and celebrates action—not just outcomes.

> If you didn't feel abundant, don't shame yourself—*observe.* Awareness breeds evolution.

3. Letting Go Practice

Write or speak the worries you're releasing for the night. You can even say: *"I release this and trust the unfolding."*

> Sleep is a manifestation portal. Clear your energy to receive insights while you rest.

Tips for Success

- **Keep it short and sacred.** 5–10 minutes is enough.
- **Pair rituals with existing anchors.** Say affirmations in the shower. Journal with your tea.
- **Use audio reminders.** Record your voice speaking affirmations and listen before bed.

Closing Reflection: Rituals Create Reality

Your habits *signal who you believe you are*. Each affirmation, each breath, each journal entry whispers to your subconscious: *I am someone who receives, sustains, and multiplies wealth.*

You're not just manifesting. You're *remembering*. And these rituals are your daily bridge back to that truth.

Morning + Evening Ritual Tracker

Daily Wealth Ritual Tracker

Day	Morning Rituals	Done ✅	Evening Rituals	
Mon	Gratitude for 3 things related to abundance 10-min visualization of wealth goals Wealth affirmation aloud	☐	Reflect on wealth wins (big or small) Journal 1 money insight Night-time affirmation	☐
Tue	Repeat above or customize	☐	Repeat above or customize	☐
Wed	Repeat above or customize	☐	Repeat above or customize	☐
Thu	Repeat above or customize	☐	Repeat above or customize	☐
Fri	Repeat above or customize	☐	Repeat above or customize	☐
Sat	Wealth-focused meditation Set financial intention for the weekend	☐	Celebrate weekly wins Affirm: "Money flows to me freely and often"	☐
Sun	Rest + realignment check-in	☐	Light journaling: "What	☐

Day	Morning Rituals	Done ✅	Evening Rituals
	Review manifestation goals		wealth came into my life this week?"

Chapter 8: *From Wishful to Wealthy: Building a Manifestation Habit That Sticks*

Anyone can make a vision board. Anyone can write an affirmation. But not everyone can *hold the vision through uncertainty, revisit their rituals when doubt creeps in*, or *choose belief when results aren't instant.*

This chapter is about becoming that person.

Manifestation isn't a quick fix. It's not a viral trend or a moon cycle ritual that fades with your feed. It's a daily alignment practice—a way of living, perceiving, and acting that reshapes your reality over time.

This is how you turn hope into habit, and habit into *your new normal.*

The Illusion of Instant Magic

One of the biggest obstacles to manifestation success is unrealistic expectations.

We live in a world of dopamine-driven gratification: 24-hour shipping, 30-second TikToks, instant likes. But wealth—real, lasting, identity-rooted wealth—is not a vending machine.

> *"Where's my money?"* you ask after three days of journaling.

But manifestation isn't about how fast it works. It's about how *deeply you embody it.*

The shift happens *when you stop asking if it's working—and decide that you are.*

The Compound Effect of Consistency

The most magnetic people aren't doing wild rituals. They're doing *simple things consistently*:

- Morning gratitude before checking notifications
- Daily action toward income goals—even small ones
- Reframing limiting beliefs *in real time*, not just in crisis
- Choosing regulation over reaction

This is *identity-level alignment*. When rituals become reflexes, your outer life has no choice but to evolve.

> **Success isn't born of intensity. It's born of intentional repetition.**

Embedding the Habit: The 3-Phase Method

Here's how to make your manifestation habit *stick*.

1. Ritualize It

Attach your practices to existing anchors:

- Mirror affirmations while brushing your teeth
- Gratitude journaling with your morning coffee
- Visualize in the shower or on your commute

You're not creating *more tasks*. You're weaving intention into what's already happening.

> *Bonus Tip:* Habit stack with rewards—light a candle, play music, make it feel *rich*.

2. Track Behavior, Not Just Results

Outcomes can take time. But behavior builds identity.

Create a tracker for:

- Daily money mantras
- Weekly aligned actions
- Emotional regulation wins

Don't ask: "Did the money come?"
Ask: *"Did I show up like someone who receives it?"*

3. Reflect + Refine Monthly

Set a ritual check-in:

- What's feeling potent?
- What's become automatic?
- What needs re-inviting?

Manifestation isn't about rigid systems—it's about responsive structure. Adjust with grace, not judgment.

Rewiring Identity: The True Manifestation Habit

The ultimate goal isn't to *do manifestation*. It's to *become the type of person* who doesn't need to question if it's working—because it's how they live, think, and breathe.

That means:

- You speak wealth even when the numbers wobble
- You give generously even when it's scary
- You celebrate the small wins as proof, not placeholders

You become so practiced in wealth identity that anything less feels foreign.

Closing Reflection: Manifestation is a Lifestyle, Not a Hack

Wishful thinking is passive.
Wealth embodiment is *proactive*.

Every time you align your thoughts, emotions, and actions—you send a signal:
"This is who I am now. This is what I'm available for."

Let others manifest sporadically.
You? You compound it daily.

Chapter 9: The Role of Patience, Timing, and Trust in Abundance

A mindset-shifting chapter for those discouraged by delays; reframing divine timing and energetic preparation.

"Delay is not denial. It's divine choreography."

In a culture of instant gratification, patience can feel like failure. When you're affirming, visualizing, journaling, and taking aligned action—yet wealth seems to tiptoe just out of reach—it's easy to question if you're doing something wrong. But here's the truth:

Manifestation operates on energy, not ego. On alignment, not urgency.

Trusting the Gestation Period

Just as a seed needs time to take root beneath the soil before it sprouts, **your wealth manifestations require an incubation phase**—a sacred period where invisible forces are rearranging your reality in ways you can't fully see yet.

You wouldn't dig up a seed every day to check if it's sprouting. Likewise, **obsessing over "when" blocks the flow of "how."** It shifts your energy from trust to scarcity, from magnetism to resistance.

Divine Timing vs. Human Timelines

Divine timing isn't always convenient, but it's always perfect. The universe works like a GPS: you set the destination, but the route recalibrates based on your alignment, growth, and unseen variables.

Sometimes the delay is protecting you. Sometimes it's preparing you. Always, it's redirecting you toward what's even better.

Instead of asking, *"Why is it taking so long?"* try:
"Who am I becoming during this process?"

Because wealth is not just what you attract. It's what you embody.

The Art of Energetic Preparation

Manifestation isn't about snapping your fingers—it's about **matching the vibration of the thing you desire**. While it's on its way, the universe invites you to become the version of yourself who can hold that abundance with grace, confidence, and purpose.

Ask yourself:

- Am I emotionally prepared to receive more?
- Do I trust myself to manage and multiply wealth?
- Have I created space—for new opportunities, for bold ideas, for the version of me that says yes to more?

This is not passive waiting. It's **active preparation**. The difference between wishing and embodying.

Ritual: The Waiting Well Practice

Create a sacred ritual to anchor your trust during uncertain periods.

1. Sit quietly with a candle or crystal symbolizing abundance.
2. Say aloud: *"Even in the waiting, I am becoming."*
3. Journal what you're learning, noticing, or being guided toward.
4. Close with gratitude for what's already on its way.

Repeat anytime your faith wobbles.

Key Takeaway:
The timing of your manifestation is not punishment—it's precision. What's for you can't miss you. Keep aligning, keep becoming, keep trusting.

Chapter 10: *Your Wealth Identity: Becoming the Version of You Who Has It All*

Manifestation starts with desire—but it *sustains* through identity. You don't manifest what you want. You manifest who you believe you are.

Most people try to change their finances while staying loyal to their old self-image: the "struggling artist," the "bad with numbers" type, the "not lucky with money" story. But wealth doesn't respond to the hustle of contradiction. It responds to *congruence*—when your self-concept aligns with your financial goals.

This chapter isn't about faking it. It's about *re-coding your identity to become the kind of person who receives and retains abundance*. Because when your inner world changes, your outer world must follow.

The Self-Concept Loop

Your self-concept is the internal story you live by. It forms through:

- Repetition of thoughts
- Emotional experiences

- Cultural conditioning
- Childhood patterns

These beliefs become a filter: You don't just interpret the world through them—you *act through them*, and the world mirrors that back.

> *If you see yourself as broke, you'll unconsciously make choices that reinforce it.*
> *If you see yourself as worthy of overflow, you'll act accordingly.*

It's not magic. It's neuroscience: identity drives behavior, and behavior creates results.

Who Is Your Wealthiest Self?

Close your eyes and meet them:

- How do they speak?
- What are their standards?
- How do they handle money decisions—big or small?
- What do they believe they deserve?

> Wealth identity isn't about luxury brands or designer bags. It's about *embodied confidence, emotional generosity, and powerful decisions*.

The version of you who "has it all" isn't flawless. They're just *anchored*. Clear. Rooted. Resourced.

Why Identity Work Works

Here's what most financial strategies ignore: If your current identity contradicts your goal, you'll sabotage it—or find it unsustainable.

- You hit a £10k month… and overspend out of guilt.
- You land your dream client… and undercharge.
- You receive praise… and deflect it.

That's not a strategy issue. It's a self-concept ceiling.

The solution? Shift your identity *first*, then let your actions flow from there.

Daily Identity Anchoring Rituals

To become your Wealth Identity, you must *spend time with them.* These tools help:

1. Mirror Identity Statements

Stand facing the mirror, eye to eye, and affirm:

- "I am the kind of person who creates financial stability with ease."
- "My decisions reflect wealth, not worry."
- "Abundance isn't a goal. It's my baseline."

Say it until it feels *familiar*, not forced.

2. Wealth Embodiment Walks

Take 10 minutes to walk as your Wealth Identity. Shoulders back. Breathing deep. Imagine you've just hit your next money milestone.

How would you move? Think? Smile?

The body doesn't lie. Embodiment rewires belief faster than words.

3. Aligned Action Audits

Ask daily: *"What action would my Wealth Identity take today?"* Then take one step—however small. The goal isn't perfection. It's congruence.

The Energetics of "Already There"

When you *become* the person who has it, you stop chasing. You magnetize.

From this identity:

- You trust the money is coming, so you stop micromanaging.
- You invest in yourself because you *know* the ROI.
- You attract aligned opportunities—because you stopped tolerating crumbs.

You don't wait for evidence. *You become the evidence.*

Closing Reflection: Your Future Self is You—Upgraded

The version of you who has it all? They're not far away. They're not more talented. They're not lucky. They're *aligned.*

You don't have to become someone else to be wealthy. You only have to stop pretending you're not.

So today, choose it. Walk like it. Decide like it. Receive like it.

Because once you shift your identity, abundance has no choice but to catch up.

Wealth Identity Blueprint

"We don't manifest what we want. We manifest who we are."

Instructions: Use this blueprint to craft, clarify, and integrate your wealth identity—so it becomes your new energetic baseline.

Step 1: Define Your Wealth Archetype

Think of the version of you who already lives with abundance. Who are they?

- Name your Wealth Identity (e.g., The Empowered Creator, The Magnetic Visionary):

  ____

- 3 traits your Wealth Identity embodies:

  ______________ • ______________ •

  ____

- Describe their energy in one sentence:

  ____

  ____

Step 2: Align Beliefs + Thoughts

Old beliefs that no longer serve this identity:

- "______________________________

  ______________________________"
- "______________________________

  ________" ______________________

New beliefs your Wealth Identity holds:

- "____
  ____
- "____
  ____"

Daily mantra:

"I am ______________________________,
and abundance is my natural state."

Step 3: Dress the Part

What does your Wealth Identity wear, carry, display?

- Clothing or accessories:
  ____
- Space/Environment upgrades:
  ____
- Symbols of wealth (objects, scents, colors):
  ____

Step 4: Speak & Move Like Them

- How does your Wealth Identity speak about money?
  ____
  ____
- How do they walk into a room?
  ____
  ____
- What's one action they would take this week that you're ready to try?
  ____

Step 5: Anchor Into Daily Life

Create 3 daily micro-habits to reinforce your identity:

1. Morning:
   ____
   ____
2. Midday:
   ____
   ____
3. Evening:
   ____
   ____

Step 6: Integration Check-In

At the end of the week, reflect:

- What felt natural?
  ____
  ____
- What felt like a stretch?
  ____
  ____
- How did your energy shift?
  ____
  ____

This worksheet gives you more than a mindset—**it gives you a mirror and a map**.

designed to help your readers not only attract abundance—but *preserve and expand it* with intention and integrity.

Chapter 11: *Wealth Boundaries – Protecting the Flow You've Created*

"Energy leaks are wealth leaks."

You've done the inner work. You've shifted beliefs, taken aligned action, and opened yourself up to receiving abundance. But just like wealth flows in—**it can flow out if not protected.** Enter: *wealth boundaries.*

Wealth isn't just about how much you attract—it's about how well you **channel, direct, and guard** that energy. Think of boundaries as sacred containers. They're what keep your flow steady, your mindset clean, and your growth sustainable.

Why Boundaries Matter in Wealth Building

Without boundaries:

- You say yes to obligations that deplete your energy (and time = money).
- You lend money from guilt rather than aligned generosity.
- You underprice your work to avoid discomfort.
- You feel resentful of others who "drain" you.

With boundaries:

- You reclaim your time and creative space.
- You stay energetically sovereign over your finances.
- You teach others how to engage with your value.

Boundaries = Self-Respect in Action.

3 Types of Wealth Boundaries You Need

1. Energetic Boundaries

Protect your time, peace, and focus.

- Practice saying *"Let me get back to you"* instead of impulsive yeses.
- Carve out wealth-focused time blocks each week.
- Minimize exposure to scarcity-driven conversations or media.

2. Emotional Boundaries
Detach your self-worth from your net worth.

- Notice when guilt or fear is driving financial decisions.
- Don't internalize others' money struggles as your responsibility.
- Affirm: *"I can be generous and still prioritize my wealth path."*

3. Financial Boundaries
Build habits that guard the flow you've created.

- Set firm limits on lending or financial favors.
- Create spending buffers that honor future-you.
- Have open, honest conversations about money in relationships.

Wealth Boundary Ritual

Try this weekly check-in:

1. What (or who) drained me financially or energetically this week?
2. What boundary would protect me from that moving forward?
3. What micro-boundary can I set this week (a "no," a limit, a restructure)?
4. What am I saying YES to by honoring that boundary?

Remember: Boundaries aren't about separation—they're about *alignment.* You're not cutting off abundance—you're ensuring it flows to where it's most valued.

Key Takeaway:
The wealth you attract is precious. The wealth you protect is powerful. Steward it wisely.

Chapter 12: Unlocking the Twelfth Gate

There comes a moment in every soul's wealth journey when striving dissolves, when affirmations echo back not as desires but as realities. The Twelfth Gate is not a physical place. It is a state of remembrance—a sacred return to the truth that you were never separate from abundance. This chapter is not about gaining more. It is about *remembering who you are.*

The Final Threshold

For eleven chapters, you've been aligning, releasing, expanding. You've written your intentions, visualized your ideal future, cultivated gratitude, reprogrammed scarcity, and embraced inspired action. Now, you stand before the final threshold—not as someone who needs to manifest wealth, but as one who has become its vessel. The Twelfth Gate opens when you no longer chase abundance… but let it move *through* you.

This gate is not unlocked by force. It opens by surrendering the last illusion: that wealth is external. That you must prove your worth. That you are somehow apart from the source. The truth is simpler and more radical—you *are* the source expressing itself as form.

Dissolving the Illusion of Separation

Many never walk through this gate because they cling to one final barrier: the belief that they are not enough. This chapter invites you to dissolve that shadow. Gently. Courageously.

Reflect: who taught you that wealth required struggle? What inner voice still whispers "not yet"? Can you recognize it with compassion, and then lovingly release it?

As you do, you reclaim your wholeness. Your birthright. You realize that the river of abundance flows not to you, but from you. And from this state, the material inevitably reshapes itself around your energetic truth.

Practicing Spiritual Affluence

Now, your task is no longer to "do" wealth—but to *be* it. To notice the endless, invisible riches already swirling through your days: easeful conversations, intuitive nudges, unexpected laughter, breathtaking light. Wealth is no longer measured only in currency, but in *connection*, *clarity*, and *creative flow*.

Here's a simple daily practice: Each morning, before speaking to the world, speak to your wealth-conscious self. Close your eyes and say aloud:

> "I walk through the Twelfth Gate with grace. I am the flow of abundance, effortlessly expressed. Today, I let wealth be who I am."

Then take one action that reflects that state. Not because you "should," but because you *can*—because it aligns with the truth you've now fully claimed.

The Integration

Let this final chapter of preparation be your integration, not an ending. The 100 manifestations you'll work with in the next section are not about attracting wealth from outside. They are spiritual scaffolding, preparing you to uncover what was always within.

You are not becoming abundant.
You *are* abundance, remembering itself.

So walk forward now, through the Twelfth Gate.
And let life reveal just how rich you already are.

Part Two

Affirmations Focused on Attracting Wealth

100 wealth focused manifestations

Here are 100 wealth-focused meditations designed to reshape mindset, strengthen financial discipline, and foster abundance.

FORWARD

Manifestation is the practice of bringing your desires into reality through focused intention, belief, and action. It operates on the principle that our thoughts and emotions shape our experiences, influencing the opportunities and outcomes we attract. For centuries, visionaries and successful individuals have harnessed this powerful technique to cultivate abundance, wealth, and personal fulfillment.

What makes manifestation so transformative is its ability to align your subconscious mind with your conscious aspirations. When practiced consistently, it rewires your thinking, strengthens your confidence, and opens pathways you may not have previously noticed. By embedding positive expectations into your daily life, you create an energetic shift that draws prosperity toward you.

To maximize the effectiveness of your manifestations:

- **Timing:** Mornings are ideal for setting the tone for the day, while evenings allow for reflection and reinforcement. Choosing moments of calm ensures deeper impact.
- **Frequency:** Reviewing and reaffirming your manifestations daily strengthens your belief and commitment.
- **Method:** Speak them aloud, write them down, or visualize them vividly—choose what resonates with you.
- **Emotion:** Infuse your manifestations with genuine excitement and gratitude to amplify their energy.

The subconscious mind is a powerful force in shaping our reality. While our conscious thoughts direct our daily decisions, our subconscious beliefs operate beneath the surface, influencing our habits, perceptions, and the energy we project into the world.

Imagine the subconscious as a vast reservoir of thoughts and emotions that continuously process information, even when we aren't actively aware of it. When we consistently focus on a desire—whether it's financial success, personal fulfillment, or a meaningful goal—our subconscious absorbs these repeated signals and begins aligning our actions, attitudes, and opportunities accordingly.

Here's why this is so powerful:

- **Belief Reinforcement:** The subconscious cannot distinguish between reality and imagination. When we visualize success with conviction, our subconscious accepts it as truth, reinforcing confidence and attracting experiences that align with this belief.
- **Pattern Recognition:** The subconscious is wired to notice patterns and opportunities that match our expectations. This is why people who believe in abundance often see wealth-generating possibilities where others see limitations.
- **Behavior Shaping:** By embedding a desired outcome into our subconscious, we instinctively make choices that bring us closer to it—often without realizing we're doing it.

To activate this process, repetition is key. Daily affirmations, visualization, and emotional investment accelerate the shift, transforming your mindset from wishful thinking into certainty. When your subconscious fully embraces your desires, it becomes a magnet for the reality you seek.

The manifestations in this book are designed to elevate your mindset and transform your financial reality. Approach them with openness, consistency, and determination, and watch wealth flow effortlessly into your life.

CONTENTS

PART ONE

Mindset for Wealth (1-25)

1. "I am worthy of financial abundance."
2. "Money flows to me effortlessly and consistently."
3. "I see opportunity everywhere I look."
4. "I release limiting beliefs about wealth."
5. "I attract prosperity in every area of my life."
6. "My financial success is inevitable."
7. "The universe is filled with unlimited wealth, and I am aligned with it."
8. "I welcome financial growth with open arms."
9. "I am confident in my ability to generate wealth."
10. "Money is a tool that allows me to live fully and generously."
11. "I deserve to be financially free."
12. "My thoughts shape my financial reality."
13. "I am grateful for all the wealth coming into my life."
14. "I make powerful and profitable financial decisions."
15. "I align my actions with abundance."
16. "Success and wealth are my natural state."
17. "Every day, I make progress toward financial independence."
18. "I embrace wise money habits that build prosperity."
19. "I use money wisely to create more freedom."

20."My wealth allows me to make a positive impact."
21."Financial abundance is my birthright."
22."My mind is focused on prosperity."
23."I take intentional steps toward financial growth."
24."I attract lucrative opportunities with ease."
25."I let go of financial fear and embrace unlimited wealth."

Financial Discipline & Action (26-50)

26."Every dollar I earn is a seed for greater abundance."
27."I invest wisely and confidently."
28."I spend mindfully, knowing my wealth is growing."
29."My financial success is built on strategic decisions."
30."I save and invest to create lasting wealth."
31."I am in control of my financial future."
32."I use money to build assets, not just expenses."
33."My money works for me even when I sleep."
34."I embrace learning about investing and wealth-building."
35."I am committed to growing my financial knowledge."
36."I welcome smart risks that lead to financial rewards."
37."I understand that wealth is built through patience and consistency."
38."I create multiple sources of income with confidence."
39."I surround myself with financially intelligent people."
40."I trust myself to make profitable financial decisions."
41."I am a wealth creator, not just a wealth consumer."
42."The actions I take today will shape my financial future."
43."I see challenges as opportunities to grow wealth."
44."Financial discipline leads to lasting abundance."
45."I manage money with wisdom and strategy."
46."Every investment I make moves me toward financial freedom."
47."I am fearless in taking financial opportunities."
48."I embrace prosperity by making smart money moves."

49."My financial habits align with my goals."
50."I create the financial life I desire with intentional choices."

Attracting Opportunities & Abundance (51-75)

51."Opportunities to create wealth present themselves daily."
52."I am open to unexpected financial blessings."
53."I attract high-value opportunities effortlessly."
54."I say yes to opportunities that align with abundance."
55."Money-making ideas flow to me with ease."
56."I trust that wealth is coming my way."
57."The universe rewards my financial confidence."
58."I radiate abundance, and wealth follows me."
59."Every financial decision I make aligns with prosperity."
60."I allow wealth to flow to me naturally."
61."I am magnetic to success and financial abundance."
62."I always find creative ways to make money."
63."I welcome unexpected financial breakthroughs."
64."My energy attracts profitable opportunities."
65."I take bold actions that lead to financial gain."
66."The wealth I desire is already on its way to me."
67."I open doors to new financial possibilities."
68."I trust in my ability to create wealth."
69."I manifest financial success through action and belief."
70."Every connection I make brings potential for financial growth."
71."I am confident in my ability to generate wealth effortlessly."
72."I trust the flow of financial prosperity into my life."
73."I am always at the right place at the right time for financial success."
74."I seize opportunities to create wealth with confidence."
75."I welcome prosperity into my life joyfully."

Living Wealth Consciously (76-100)

76."My wealth expands as I give generously."
77."I use money to enrich my life and the lives of others."
78."Abundance allows me to contribute to meaningful causes."
79."I make financial decisions that reflect my values."
80."My wealth supports my dreams and passions."
81."I practice gratitude for every financial blessing."
82."I respect and honor money by using it wisely."
83."I align my spending with wealth-building principles."
84."I make financial choices from a place of confidence, not fear."
85."I am in harmony with the flow of financial abundance."
86."I use wealth as a force for good in my life and community."
87."My prosperity creates security and freedom."
88."I manage wealth responsibly and intentionally."
89."I create financial stability that benefits my future generations."
90."My financial growth fuels my personal and professional success."
91."I enjoy the process of wealth-building."
92."I celebrate my financial achievements, big and small."
93."My wealth allows me to live life on my own terms."
94."I use financial wisdom to make empowered choices."
95."The more I learn about wealth, the more I attract abundance."
96."I am a leader in financial empowerment."
97."Financial success is a reflection of my growth and mindset."
98."I build wealth in alignment with my highest purpose."
99."I welcome limitless prosperity into my life."
100."My financial future is bright, abundant, and secure."

PART TWO

ACTIONS TO REINFORCE THE MANIFESTATIONS

These meditations work best when paired with action—mindset alone isn't enough, but belief drives behavior! Here are 100 wealth-focused meditations, each paired with a practical action to reinforce the mindset and translate intention into results.

Mindset for Wealth (1-25)

1. "I am worthy of financial abundance." → **Action:** Write down 3 reasons why you deserve financial success.
2. "Money flows to me effortlessly and consistently." → **Action:** Set up an automatic savings plan or investment contribution.
3. "I see opportunity everywhere I look." → **Action:** Find and research one new investment or business idea today.
4. "I release limiting beliefs about wealth." → **Action:** Identify a belief that holds you back and replace it with an empowering truth.
5. "I attract prosperity in every area of my life." → **Action:** Make a gratitude list focusing on financial opportunities in your life.
6. "My financial success is inevitable." → **Action:** Visualize what financial success looks like for you.
7. "The universe is filled with unlimited wealth, and I am aligned with it." → **Action:** Learn about a financial opportunity you hadn't considered before.
8. "I welcome financial growth with open arms." → **Action:** Invest time in financial education through a book, podcast, or course.
9. "I am confident in my ability to generate wealth." → **Action:** Take the first step toward an income-generating

project.

10. "Money is a tool that allows me to live fully and generously." → **Action:** Plan a budget that supports wealth-building and generosity.
11. "I deserve to be financially free." → **Action:** Define what financial freedom looks like and set one goal toward achieving it.
12. "My thoughts shape my financial reality." → **Action:** Monitor your daily thoughts about money and shift negative ones into positive beliefs.
13. "I am grateful for all the wealth coming into my life." → **Action:** List five financial blessings you already have.
14. "I make powerful and profitable financial decisions." → **Action:** Analyze your next financial decision with confidence and strategy.
15. "I align my actions with abundance." → **Action:** Stop engaging in one habit that keeps you financially stagnant.
16. "Success and wealth are my natural state." → **Action:** Dress and present yourself in a way that reflects your future wealthy self.
17. "Every day, I make progress toward financial independence." → **Action:** Take one small financial action today, no matter how minor.
18. "I embrace wise money habits that build prosperity." → **Action:** Track all expenses for a week to see patterns in spending.
19. "I use money wisely to create more freedom." → **Action:** Redirect unnecessary spending toward investments or savings.
20. "My wealth allows me to make a positive impact." → **Action:** Donate or contribute to a cause aligned with your financial success.
21. "Financial abundance is my birthright." → **Action:** Say this affirmation aloud every morning.

22. "My mind is focused on prosperity." → **Action:** Eliminate distractions preventing financial growth and focus on wealth-building activities.
23. "I take intentional steps toward financial growth." → **Action:** Create a written financial roadmap for the next five years.
24. "I attract lucrative opportunities with ease." → **Action:** Connect with a mentor or network with successful individuals.
25. "I let go of financial fear and embrace unlimited wealth." → **Action:** List your biggest financial fear and write down ways to overcome it.

(And so on—each meditation has its corresponding action.)

This structure ensures that your mindset aligns with tangible steps toward wealth-building.

Here are the next 25 actions to accompany the wealth-focused meditations:

Financial Discipline & Action (26-50)

26. "Every dollar I earn is a seed for greater abundance." → **Action:** Set aside a portion of every income source for investing.
27. "I invest wisely and confidently." → **Action:** Research an investment option and commit to learning its basics.
28. "I spend mindfully, knowing my wealth is growing." → **Action:** Analyze your recent purchases and identify wasteful spending.
29. "My financial success is built on strategic decisions." → **Action:** Make a financial plan with long-term goals in mind.
30. "I save and invest to create lasting wealth." → **Action:** Automate a percentage of your income into a savings or

investment account.

31."I am in control of my financial future." → **Action:** Set up financial tracking tools to monitor your net worth.

32."I use money to build assets, not just expenses." → **Action:** Start prioritizing asset-building purchases over liabilities.

33."My money works for me even when I sleep." → **Action:** Explore passive income streams that can generate earnings over time.

34."I embrace learning about investing and wealth-building." → **Action:** Read or listen to a financial book, podcast, or expert talk this week.

35."I am committed to growing my financial knowledge." → **Action:** Join a financial education group or online forum.

36."I welcome smart risks that lead to financial rewards." → **Action:** Take a calculated risk in an investment or business venture.

37."I understand that wealth is built through patience and consistency." → **Action:** Commit to long-term financial habits rather than seeking quick wins.

38."I create multiple sources of income with confidence." → **Action:** Brainstorm and execute on a new side income stream.

39."I surround myself with financially intelligent people." → **Action:** Connect with a mentor or wealth-minded community.

40."I trust myself to make profitable financial decisions." → **Action:** Take ownership of a financial choice today without fear or hesitation.

41."I am a wealth creator, not just a wealth consumer." → **Action:** Focus more on producing value than spending on consumption.

42."The actions I take today will shape my financial future." → **Action:** Make one decision that brings you closer to financial independence.

43."I see challenges as opportunities to grow wealth." → **Action:** Identify a financial setback and create a plan to overcome it.

44."Financial discipline leads to lasting abundance." → **Action:** Set strict financial boundaries to eliminate unnecessary expenses.

45."I manage money with wisdom and strategy." → **Action:** Review and adjust your budgeting system for efficiency.

46."Every investment I make moves me toward financial freedom." → **Action:** Assess your investment portfolio and make improvements.

47."I am fearless in taking financial opportunities." → **Action:** Take action on an opportunity you've been hesitant about.

48."I embrace prosperity by making smart money moves." → **Action:** Avoid impulse spending and align purchases with long-term goals.

49."My financial habits align with my goals." → **Action:** Compare your habits with your goals and refine them accordingly.

50."I create the financial life I desire with intentional choices." → **Action:** Decide on your ideal financial future and take a step toward it today.

Attracting Opportunities & Abundance (51-75)

51."Opportunities to create wealth present themselves daily." → **Action:** Identify one opportunity today and take action on it.

52."I am open to unexpected financial blessings." → **Action:** Keep an open mind—say yes to a new financial opportunity.

53."I attract high-value opportunities effortlessly." → **Action:**

Expand your network to connect with influential or knowledgeable people.

54. "I say yes to opportunities that align with abundance." → **Action:** Filter opportunities based on long-term wealth-building potential.
55. "Money-making ideas flow to me with ease." → **Action:** Write down five potential income-generating ideas and evaluate them.
56. "I trust that wealth is coming my way." → **Action:** Let go of fear and take a financial step forward with confidence.
57. "The universe rewards my financial confidence." → **Action:** Approach financial decisions with self-trust and decisiveness.
58. "I radiate abundance, and wealth follows me." → **Action:** Present yourself confidently and communicate with a wealth mindset.
59. "Every financial decision I make aligns with prosperity." → **Action:** Review upcoming financial decisions and ensure they support growth.
60. "I allow wealth to flow to me naturally." → **Action:** Remove financial resistance—invest without overanalyzing.
61. "I am magnetic to success and financial abundance." → **Action:** Align daily actions with your financial goals.
62. "I always find creative ways to make money." → **Action:** Explore unconventional income streams that align with your skills.
63. "I welcome unexpected financial breakthroughs." → **Action:** Look for small wins—extra income, discounts, or unexpected savings.
64. "My energy attracts profitable opportunities." → **Action:** Position yourself where high-value opportunities emerge.
65. "I take bold actions that lead to financial gain." → **Action:** Make a financial move today that pushes you outside your

comfort zone.

66."The wealth I desire is already on its way to me." → **Action:** Set up financial systems that create passive income.

67."I open doors to new financial possibilities." → **Action:** Explore industries or investment areas beyond your usual scope.

68."I trust in my ability to create wealth." → **Action:** Take initiative in a wealth-building opportunity without hesitation.

69."I manifest financial success through action and belief." → **Action:** Make decisions based on abundance, not scarcity.

70."Every connection I make brings potential for financial growth." → **Action:** Strengthen relationships with people who inspire financial success.

71."I am confident in my ability to generate wealth effortlessly." → **Action:** Begin automating financial decisions for long-term stability.

72."I trust the flow of financial prosperity into my life." → **Action:** Recognize where abundance already exists and build on it.

73."I am always at the right place at the right time for financial success." → **Action:** Be proactive—seek knowledge, events, and conversations that lead to wealth.

74."I seize opportunities to create wealth with confidence." → **Action:** Stop hesitating—commit to an investment, business move, or smart financial choice today.

75."I welcome prosperity into my life joyfully." → **Action:** Express gratitude for every financial improvement, no matter how small.

Living Wealth Consciously (76-100)

76. "My wealth expands as I give generously." → **Action:** Make a small donation or support a cause that aligns with your values.
77. "I use money to enrich my life and the lives of others." → **Action:** Allocate a portion of your wealth toward meaningful experiences or helping others.
78. "Abundance allows me to contribute to meaningful causes." → **Action:** Identify a cause or charity that resonates with you and support it financially or through volunteering.
79. "I make financial decisions that reflect my values." → **Action:** Ensure your spending aligns with your long-term wealth-building goals.
80. "My wealth supports my dreams and passions." → **Action:** Invest in education, travel, or personal development that enriches your life.
81. "I practice gratitude for every financial blessing." → **Action:** Write down three financial wins you've had recently, no matter how small.
82. "I respect and honor money by using it wisely." → **Action:** Avoid wasteful spending and focus on making purposeful financial choices.
83. "I align my spending with wealth-building principles." → **Action:** Prioritize investments and assets over unnecessary expenses.
84. "I make financial choices from a place of confidence, not fear." → **Action:** Stop hesitating—make that financial move you've been overthinking.
85. "I am in harmony with the flow of financial abundance." → **Action:** Let go of scarcity-driven decisions and embrace wealth-oriented thinking.
86. "I use wealth as a force for good in my life and community." → **Action:** Support an initiative or business

that promotes positive change.

87. "My prosperity creates security and freedom." → **Action:** Build an emergency fund or increase your savings for long-term stability.
88. "I manage wealth responsibly and intentionally." → **Action:** Review your financial goals and adjust your strategies accordingly.
89. "I create financial stability that benefits my future generations." → **Action:** Learn about wealth transfer strategies and long-term financial planning.
90. "My financial growth fuels my personal and professional success." → **Action:** Invest in learning and skills that enhance your earning potential.
91. "I enjoy the process of wealth-building." → **Action:** Find excitement in tracking your progress and celebrating milestones.
92. "I celebrate my financial achievements, big and small." → **Action:** Reward yourself for hitting financial goals—mindfully and responsibly.
93. "My wealth allows me to live life on my own terms." → **Action:** Take one step toward an independent financial lifestyle today.
94. "I use financial wisdom to make empowered choices." → **Action:** Double-check your financial decisions to ensure they support wealth-building.
95. "The more I learn about wealth, the more I attract abundance." → **Action:** Dedicate time to reading, studying, or engaging in financial discussions.
96. "I am a leader in financial empowerment." → **Action:** Share financial knowledge with someone who may benefit from it.
97. "Financial success is a reflection of my growth and mindset." → **Action:** Strengthen your wealth mindset through consistent learning and strategic action.

98. "I build wealth in alignment with my highest purpose." → **Action:** Ensure your financial strategies align with your deeper life goals.
99. "I welcome limitless prosperity into my life." → **Action:** Stay open to new wealth-building opportunities and act on them.
100. "My financial future is bright, abundant, and secure." → **Action:** Commit to your wealth journey and embrace financial freedom.

PART THREE

UNDERSTANDING THE POWER OF THE ACTIONS

1. "I am worthy of financial abundance."

To internalize this belief, you must first eliminate any subconscious doubts about wealth. Start by identifying limiting beliefs that tell you wealth is unattainable or reserved for others. Write them down, then counter each belief with a powerful affirmation, like "I deserve prosperity because I provide value to the world." Surround yourself with financially successful influences—whether books, mentors, or social circles—to reshape your perspective. Practicing gratitude for existing financial blessings will also reinforce your self-worth in relation to money.

2. "Money flows to me effortlessly and consistently."

Building financial consistency requires systems. Set up automatic savings and investment contributions so wealth grows without daily effort. Identify and create at least one passive income stream —this could be stock dividends, rental income, or monetizing digital assets. Align your income sources so they compound over time rather than rely on constant labor. Stay open to unexpected financial opportunities by networking and expanding your skills.

3. "I see opportunity everywhere I look."

Develop an entrepreneurial mindset by observing your surroundings with a wealth-oriented lens. Look at how businesses operate, how consumer trends shift, and where gaps exist in the market. Keep a journal where you document money-making ideas regularly, even if they seem small or unconventional. Train yourself to ask, "How can I create value here?" in every situation. Opportunities often come disguised as problems—learn to approach challenges with a solution-driven perspective.

4. "I release limiting beliefs about wealth."

Identify any negative associations you have with money—perhaps from childhood, societal conditioning, or past failures. Recognize how these beliefs might be restricting your financial growth. Challenge these thoughts through exposure to wealth-positive narratives—read autobiographies of self-made entrepreneurs, study successful investors, and listen to experts who have built financial independence. Actively practice wealth-oriented habits, such as responsible investing, budgeting, and generating multiple income streams, to rewire your thinking.

5. "I attract prosperity in every area of my life."

Start by ensuring your actions match your desires for prosperity. If wealth is your goal, ensure you make financial decisions with abundance in mind—this means investing in education, networking with financial-savvy individuals, and taking steps toward financial independence. Cultivate an environment that reinforces prosperity; declutter financial chaos by setting clear monetary goals and structuring efficient spending habits. Recognize the prosperity you already have, which may not only be financial but also intellectual and social capital that you can leverage.

6. "My financial success is inevitable."

Believing in inevitable success requires structured action. Create a wealth-building roadmap outlining where you want to be financially in 1, 5, and 10 years. Break it down into manageable steps—learning about investing, increasing your income sources, and improving financial literacy. Progressively scale your money habits so your actions align with your long-term financial vision. Execute financial decisions confidently, treating setbacks as necessary lessons rather than roadblocks.

7. "The universe is filled with unlimited wealth, and I am aligned with it."

To embody this belief, detach from scarcity thinking—the idea that money is limited or unattainable. Study examples of wealth creation across various industries to affirm that financial opportunities are abundant. Engage in environments where wealth circulation is evident—attend business events, interact with high-performing individuals, and observe thriving economies. Challenge the notion that wealth is reserved for a select few by positioning yourself within financial success narratives.

8. "I welcome financial growth with open arms."

To truly welcome financial expansion, you must be willing to step into new levels of learning, risk-taking, and execution. Make financial education a priority by committing to learning about investments, taxes, and wealth strategies. Accept opportunities that push you beyond your comfort zone—whether it's starting a side business, making your first investment, or changing your financial habits. Recognize growth not just in profits but in financial literacy, resilience, and risk management.

9. "I am confident in my ability to generate wealth."

Confidence in wealth-building comes from experience and execution. Take action daily toward financial growth, even if it’s as small as researching investments or saving money toward assets. Surround yourself with individuals who reinforce your ability to succeed financially—mentors, peers, and educators who inspire financial confidence. Set realistic financial targets and achieve them progressively to build self-trust. Avoid relying solely on job income; explore investments, business ventures, and alternative income sources.

10. "Money is a tool that allows me to live fully and generously."

Shift your mindset from viewing money as a mere necessity to recognizing it as a powerful tool for freedom, growth, and impact. Use your wealth intentionally by allocating funds toward personal development, experiences that enrich your life, and causes you believe in. Instead of spending impulsively, view every financial decision through the lens of long-term value—asking whether the expense contributes to security, freedom, or purpose. Practicing generosity also reinforces a mindset of abundance—donate, mentor, or support initiatives that elevate others financially.

Each of these actions builds a strong foundation for long-term financial success. Let me know if you'd like further refinements or expansions!

Certainly! Here's a structured approach to achieving the next 10 wealth-building manifestations with detailed actions:

11. "I deserve to be financially free."

Financial freedom starts with a decision to build wealth rather than just earn wages. Begin by defining what financial freedom means to you—whether it's having passive income that exceeds expenses, eliminating debt, or gaining full control over your time. Structure a plan to move toward financial independence by setting milestones: increasing savings, investing in assets, and diversifying income streams. Cut unnecessary financial burdens and optimize expenses to accelerate your journey toward freedom.

12. "My thoughts shape my financial reality."

Your beliefs about money influence every financial decision you make. If you think wealth is unattainable, you'll hesitate to invest or take smart risks. To shift your mindset, practice awareness—each time you have a limiting thought about money, replace it with an abundance-focused belief. Make financial affirmations a daily habit, write down specific financial goals, and surround yourself with financial education materials. The more knowledge you gain, the more confidence you'll have in your financial reality.

13. "I am grateful for all the wealth coming into my life."

Gratitude shifts focus away from scarcity and into abundance, reinforcing wealth-conscious decision-making. Keep a daily journal where you list financial wins, no matter how small—extra savings, new income sources, investment growth, or learning opportunities. Express gratitude for financial progress, even if it's not immediate wealth. Being thankful for what you already have attracts more prosperity and reduces financial anxiety.

14. "I make powerful and profitable financial decisions."

A profitable decision is backed by knowledge and foresight. Before making financial commitments, research extensively and compare multiple options. Develop a system for evaluating investments, business opportunities, and major purchases based on return potential and risk tolerance. Learn from experienced investors or entrepreneurs, and avoid emotional decision-making —stay strategic. Keep records of past decisions and analyze what worked well, adjusting your strategy accordingly.

15. "I align my actions with abundance."

Abundance requires intentional action, not just positive thinking. Take steps that align with financial prosperity: prioritize investments over unnecessary spending, seek opportunities to generate passive income, and make wealth-building a daily practice. Actively engage in wealth education—attend seminars, network with financially successful individuals, and study strategies that have helped others achieve financial success. Your behaviors must reflect the prosperity you desire.

16. "Success and wealth are my natural state."

To embody success as a natural state, act as if you are already financially independent. Adopt habits of the wealthy—learn how to manage assets, handle investments, and think in terms of long-term value rather than immediate gratification. Adjust your mindset so that financial success isn't a distant dream but an expectation based on consistent actions. Make decisions that set you up for future prosperity, rather than staying trapped in paycheck-to-paycheck thinking.

17. "Every day, I make progress toward financial independence."

Financial freedom is a gradual process, achieved through daily actions. Break down wealth-building into manageable steps: automate savings, reduce wasteful spending, make educated financial decisions, and continuously learn about investments. Track your progress weekly or monthly and celebrate small victories. Whether you open a new investment account, learn a new financial concept, or increase passive income, every step contributes to your independence.

18. "I embrace wise money habits that build prosperity."

Wealth is built on strong financial habits. To develop wise money practices, review your spending patterns and optimize cash flow management. Learn how to allocate money efficiently—ensuring that more goes into assets rather than liabilities. Adopt habits such as tracking expenses, reducing debt strategically, and making calculated investments. The more disciplined your financial behavior, the more wealth you will accumulate over time.

19. "I use money wisely to create more freedom."

Every financial decision should contribute to long-term freedom, not short-term gratification. Prioritize purchases and investments based on how they enhance financial independence—buy assets that generate income instead of liabilities that drain wealth. Consider automation tools that grow wealth effortlessly, such as automated investments and passive income systems. Redirect unnecessary spending toward ventures that support financial growth.

20. "My wealth allows me to make a positive impact."

True wealth is not just accumulation—it's about contribution and empowerment. As you grow financially, look for ways to use wealth to improve your life and the lives of others. Invest in initiatives that align with your values, support businesses that uplift communities, and educate others on financial independence. Creating impact strengthens your relationship with money and reinforces the principle that financial growth benefits both you and society.

These detailed steps ensure each manifestation is backed by intentional action, reinforcing financial progress. Let me know if you'd like further refinements or expansions!

Of course! Here's a detailed breakdown of actions for the next 20 wealth-building manifestations:

Financial Discipline & Strategic Action (21-40)

21. "Financial abundance is my birthright."

To embrace this truth, eliminate scarcity thinking and view wealth as something attainable, not exclusive. Research how self-made individuals built financial security, proving that wealth is accessible through knowledge and strategy. Set clear financial goals and act with confidence—whether it's starting an investment portfolio, launching a business, or increasing savings.

22. "My mind is focused on prosperity."

Train your brain to consistently seek financial growth. Limit distractions and prioritize wealth-building activities, such as learning about money management, refining financial strategies, and networking with financially successful individuals. Create a vision board displaying your financial targets to keep prosperity top of mind.

23. "I take intentional steps toward financial growth."

Every financial decision should contribute to long-term prosperity. Regularly review your financial progress and refine strategies to improve cash flow. Ensure each income stream—whether active or passive—aligns with stability and growth. Start investing consistently, even in small amounts, to create compounding wealth.

24. "I attract lucrative opportunities with ease."

To welcome high-value financial opportunities, engage with thriving industries, expand your network, and position yourself where wealth-building conversations happen. Instead of waiting for opportunities, actively seek investment openings, business ventures, or skill-based revenue streams.

25. "I let go of financial fear and embrace unlimited wealth."

Recognizing fear-based money habits is key to breaking barriers. Whether it's avoiding investment due to risk or hesitating on financial ventures, acknowledge the fear but don't let it control you. Gradually take calculated financial steps toward investment and entrepreneurship, trusting in your ability to make sound decisions.

26. "Every dollar I earn is a seed for greater abundance."

Shift spending habits from consumption to wealth-building. Allocate every income source efficiently—designating portions for saving, investing, and reinvestment in skill development. Avoid spending solely based on lifestyle; instead, focus on multiplying income.

27. "I invest wisely and confidently."

Study investment strategies, evaluate risk-reward balances, and make informed financial decisions. Choose assets aligned with your goals, whether it's stocks, real estate, or businesses. Commit to consistency, as wealth accumulation thrives on long-term investing.

28. "I spend mindfully, knowing my wealth is growing."

Avoid financial leaks by analyzing spending habits and eliminating unnecessary expenses. Before making purchases, ask yourself whether they contribute to financial security or long-term wealth creation. Redirect savings toward high-yield investments.

29. "My financial success is built on strategic decisions."

Stop making impulsive financial moves. Instead, evaluate investments, business opportunities, and major purchases thoroughly. Establish financial principles that guide every decision—ensuring they align with wealth-building rather than momentary satisfaction.

30. "I save and invest to create lasting wealth."

Implement a system where savings automatically flow into investments. Set clear benchmarks for wealth-building (e.g., accumulating a set amount in your portfolio, acquiring income-generating assets) and maintain consistency in financial commitments.

31. "I am in control of my financial future."

Take full ownership of financial decisions. Rather than relying on employment alone, develop financial literacy and cultivate income streams that are self-sustaining. Recognize that financial independence is built through deliberate choices, not chance.

32. "I use money to build assets, not just expenses."

Shift from consumer-oriented thinking to investment-driven decisions. Instead of spending on depreciating assets, such as luxury items with no return, allocate funds toward assets that generate income—property, business ventures, and stock ownership.

33. "My money works for me even when I sleep."

The wealthy build passive income through systems rather than direct labor. Establish income-generating assets, automate investments, and explore business models that create revenue with minimal daily intervention. Ensure wealth grows even in your absence.

34. "I embrace learning about investing and wealth-building."

Financial education is the cornerstone of prosperity. Study wealth-building principles, attend seminars, and engage with experienced investors. Make learning about money a lifelong commitment rather than a one-time event.

35. "I am committed to growing my financial knowledge."

Seek out expert financial books, courses, and mentorships to refine your understanding of wealth accumulation. Apply knowledge practically—adjust investment strategies based on insights gained.

36. "I welcome smart risks that lead to financial rewards."

Calculated risks are necessary for wealth-building. Evaluate opportunities carefully, ensuring they align with your financial growth strategy. Don't let fear prevent financial progress—choose informed risks that open doors to new prosperity.

37. "I understand that wealth is built through patience and consistency."

Avoid chasing instant riches—true financial success is cultivated through time, discipline, and persistence. Stick to structured investment strategies, follow through with business models, and remain committed to the long haul rather than seeking shortcuts.

38. "I create multiple sources of income with confidence."

Relying on a single paycheck can be risky, especially as industries evolve. To create multiple streams of income, start by identifying your skills, assets, and marketable opportunities. Consider diverse income avenues such as freelancing, consulting, rental properties, dividend stocks, or digital product sales. Build income streams progressively—begin with one, optimize its success, then expand. Avoid overcommitting to too many ventures at once; instead, focus on scalable sources that align with your long-term financial goals.

39. "I surround myself with financially intelligent people."

Your financial mindset is influenced by those around you. Audit your social circles and ensure you engage with people who encourage smart financial habits and wealth-building strategies. Join networking events, financial discussion forums, and mastermind groups centered on investment, entrepreneurship, and passive income. Follow reputable financial educators, listen to wealth-building podcasts, and seek mentorship from experienced investors. The more you immerse yourself in financially intelligent conversations, the more confident and strategic you'll become.

40. "I trust myself to make profitable financial decisions."

Financial confidence is built through knowledge, experience, and decisive action. Strengthen your ability to assess investments, risks, and opportunities by continuously learning—read financial books, analyze market trends, and study investment strategies. Rather than second-guessing, commit to informed decisions and refine your approach over time. Document past financial choices, evaluate what worked, and adjust based on lessons learned. The key is to trust your financial judgment while staying adaptable in an ever-changing economic landscape.

Each of these steps ensures financial growth through intentional action and smart decision-making.

Strategic Wealth Creation & Mindset Development (41-60)

41. "I am a wealth creator, not just a wealth consumer."

To shift from consuming wealth to generating it, prioritize investments over expenses. Instead of spending on luxury items, redirect those funds toward assets that appreciate, such as stocks, real estate, or businesses. Create something that brings value to others—whether a service, product, or digital resource. Developing financial literacy and reinvesting profits will solidify your role as a wealth creator.

42. "The actions I take today will shape my financial future."

Avoid procrastinating financial decisions. Start immediately—whether it's setting up an investment account, learning about tax-efficient wealth growth, or eliminating unnecessary expenses. Future prosperity depends on consistent, deliberate action today.

43. "I see challenges as opportunities to grow wealth."

Every financial setback holds a lesson. Instead of fearing difficulties, analyze challenges and find solutions—if you experience losses in an investment, refine your strategy; if income stagnates, explore new opportunities. Approach every challenge as a chance to expand financial intelligence and resilience.

44. "Financial discipline leads to lasting abundance."

Without disciplined habits, wealth disappears quickly. Automate savings, avoid impulse purchases, and structure financial planning. Hold yourself accountable by setting monthly wealth-building benchmarks and tracking your progress regularly.

45. "I manage money with wisdom and strategy."

Financial wisdom comes from understanding cash flow, investment risk, and opportunities. Create a budget aligned with long-term wealth goals, diversify investments, and ensure each financial decision contributes to stability and future prosperity.

46. "Every investment I make moves me toward financial freedom."

Evaluate each investment with a wealth-growth mindset. Before committing, research potential returns, risks, and long-term viability. Favor investments that generate passive income, allowing your money to work for you continuously.

47. "I am fearless in taking financial opportunities."

Fear often holds people back from profitable investments. Instead of hesitating, apply financial knowledge and take decisive actions. Assess risk wisely, but don't let fear prevent progress—embrace calculated wealth-building moves confidently.

48. "I embrace prosperity by making smart money moves."

Ensure financial decisions align with wealth accumulation. Instead of chasing instant gratification, focus on sustainable wealth strategies, such as long-term investments and passive income generation.

49. "My financial habits align with my goals."

Compare your daily financial behaviors with your long-term wealth objectives—if spending patterns conflict with financial independence, make adjustments immediately. Small consistent habits, like automated investing and mindful spending, accelerate wealth-building.

50. "I create the financial life I desire with intentional choices."

Develop a clear financial vision, setting specific targets for wealth, investments, and income streams. Execute each step with purpose, avoiding distractions and financial missteps.

Attracting Wealth & Opportunities (51-70)

51. "Opportunities to create wealth present themselves daily."

Actively seek financial opportunities—monitor market trends, explore new investment vehicles, and connect with individuals who offer insights into wealth-building strategies.

52. "I am open to unexpected financial blessings."

Stay adaptable in your financial journey—unforeseen opportunities, such as new collaborations or investment breakthroughs, often lead to greater prosperity. Be ready to act when they appear.

53. "I attract high-value opportunities effortlessly."

Position yourself where financial opportunities emerge—network with successful individuals, engage with wealth-building communities, and demonstrate expertise in lucrative fields.

54. "I say yes to opportunities that align with abundance."

Evaluate each financial opportunity based on long-term benefits—prioritize ventures that contribute to sustained wealth rather than short-lived gains.

55. "Money-making ideas flow to me with ease."

Cultivate an entrepreneurial mindset by brainstorming innovative ways to generate wealth. Keep a daily journal of financial ideas, explore emerging industries, and refine business strategies.

56. "I trust that wealth is coming my way."

Adopt the mindset that financial success is inevitable with the right strategies. Consistently act on wealth-building plans and remain confident in your ability to achieve financial prosperity.

57. "The universe rewards my financial confidence."

Make bold but informed decisions in investing, entrepreneurship, and career shifts. Confidence backed by financial wisdom attracts profitable opportunities and accelerates wealth accumulation.

58. "I radiate abundance, and wealth follows me."

Strengthen financial self-image—dress, speak, and act with prosperity in mind. Engage in conversations about wealth-building, and position yourself as someone aligned with financial success.

59. "Every financial decision I make aligns with prosperity."

Regularly audit financial decisions—eliminate choices that hinder wealth growth and refine strategies to maximize profitability and asset accumulation.

60. "I allow wealth to flow to me naturally."

Stop forcing financial success and instead structure income streams that generate effortless returns, such as passive investments and automated wealth-building systems.

Living Wealth Consciously & Empowerment (71-80)

71. "I am confident in my ability to generate wealth effortlessly."

Financial confidence comes from knowledge and execution—dedicate time to learning investment strategies, passive income models, and long-term financial planning.

72. "I trust the flow of financial prosperity into my life."

Develop trust in your financial decisions—review strategies that yield success and refine weaker areas, but stay committed to wealth growth without hesitation.

73. "I am always at the right place at the right time for financial success."

Strategically place yourself where wealth-building conversations and opportunities happen—attend investment seminars, network with financially educated people, and actively engage with wealth-related discussions.

74. "I seize opportunities to create wealth with confidence."

Hesitation delays financial success—commit to informed investments, execute business plans, and capitalize on money-making ventures immediately.

75. "I welcome prosperity into my life joyfully."

Approach financial success with gratitude and openness. Appreciate wealth-building progress and avoid stress-based financial decisions—abundance flourishes where optimism exists.

76. "My wealth expands as I give generously."

Strategic generosity builds a cycle of prosperity—support causes that align with financial growth, reinvest in social capital, and assist others in their wealth journeys.

77. "I use money to enrich my life and the lives of others."

Ensure financial success enhances experiences—travel, education, and philanthropy amplify wealth impact beyond personal financial stability.

78. "Abundance allows me to contribute to meaningful causes."

Allocate a portion of earnings toward impactful ventures—philanthropic investments often create long-term financial and societal benefits.

79. "I make financial decisions that reflect my values."

Align financial habits with ethical principles—support responsible investing, build wealth consciously, and ensure success benefits both you and others.

80. "My wealth supports my dreams and passions."

Structure financial planning around passions and life ambitions—channel investments and income sources toward lifestyle freedom and career fulfillment.

Living Wealth Consciously & Empowerment (81-100)

81. "I practice gratitude for every financial blessing."

Gratitude cultivates abundance. Create a daily habit of listing financial wins, whether big or small—unexpected income, smart investments, or lessons learned from financial experiences. A grateful mindset attracts more opportunities for prosperity.

82. "I respect and honor money by using it wisely."

Treat money as a tool for growth. Develop financial discipline—track expenses, optimize spending, and invest where it matters most. Avoid reckless financial decisions that diminish long-term wealth accumulation.

83. "I align my spending with wealth-building principles."

Evaluate purchases based on long-term financial goals. Prioritize assets over liabilities, investing in education, business growth, and passive income streams rather than temporary luxuries.

84. "I make financial choices from a place of confidence, not fear."

Fear-based money decisions limit growth. Study financial strategies, gain knowledge, and take decisive action without hesitation. Trust your ability to create sustainable wealth.

85. "I am in harmony with the flow of financial abundance."

Align actions with prosperity—invest wisely, manage money efficiently, and maintain financial momentum without unnecessary stress. Prosperity comes through clarity, structure, and aligned financial behavior.

86. "I use wealth as a force for good in my life and community."

Successful wealth-building extends beyond personal gain. Invest in meaningful causes, support businesses that align with ethical principles, and use financial success to create positive impact.

87. "My prosperity creates security and freedom."

True wealth ensures financial independence. Develop income streams that sustain long-term security—whether through investments, automated earnings, or well-planned savings.

88. "I manage wealth responsibly and intentionally."

Take complete ownership of your financial journey. Develop systems for budgeting, asset allocation, and strategic growth—ensuring each financial decision contributes to stability and expansion.

89. "I create financial stability that benefits future generations."

Build wealth that outlasts your lifetime. Learn about generational wealth strategies, estate planning, and investments that create financial security for years to come.

90. "My financial growth fuels my personal and professional success."

Wealth-building should complement your personal and career development. Ensure financial success aligns with professional growth, enabling opportunities for advancement, independence, and fulfillment.

91. "I enjoy the process of wealth-building."

Shift financial growth from a task to a rewarding experience. Embrace learning, refining strategies, and celebrating milestones. Prosperity thrives when the wealth-building journey is enjoyable.

92. "I celebrate my financial achievements, big and small."

Recognize progress, no matter the scale. Each financial win—whether debt reduction, successful investments, or income growth—deserves acknowledgment. Success builds upon appreciation.

93. "My wealth allows me to live life on my own terms."

Financial independence grants choices—where to work, how to spend time, and what opportunities to pursue. Ensure financial strategies align with the lifestyle you aspire to create.

94. "I use financial wisdom to make empowered choices."

Wealth is built through informed decision-making. Strengthen financial literacy, refine investment strategies, and ensure every choice moves you toward long-term financial security.

95. "The more I learn about wealth, the more I attract abundance."

Commit to financial education—consume books, courses, and expert knowledge on wealth-building. Constant learning enhances decision-making and wealth accumulation.

96. "I am a leader in financial empowerment."

Share financial wisdom with others—mentor, educate, and encourage wealth-building practices in your community. Wealth expands when financial knowledge is passed on.

97. "Financial success is a reflection of my growth and mindset."

Your financial state mirrors your mindset and habits. Strengthen wealth-oriented thinking, embrace disciplined financial behavior, and cultivate resilience in financial decision-making.

98. "I build wealth in alignment with my highest purpose."

Ensure financial success aligns with personal values and aspirations. Invest in ventures, careers, and opportunities that contribute to your long-term fulfillment beyond monetary gain.

99. "I welcome limitless prosperity into my life."

Detach from scarcity thinking—embrace wealth-building strategies that expand opportunities rather than limit potential. Stay open to financial breakthroughs.

100. "My financial future is bright, abundant, and secure."

Maintain clarity in financial planning. Structure wealth-building efforts effectively, continuously refine strategies, and remain confident in financial independence.

This final set completes the structured actions for wealth-building, ensuring financial success stems from intentional growth and empowerment.

PART FOUR -AUTHORS THAT HAVE WRITTEN ABOUT MANIFESTATIONS FOR WEALTH-BUILDING

Many authors have written extensively on wealth-building, financial independence, and mindset shifts that align with the steps we've outlined. Here are some key books and authors that provide guidance on these principles:

Mindset & Wealth Psychology

- **Napoleon Hill** – *Think and Grow Rich* (Developing a wealth-oriented mindset)
- **T. Harv Eker** – *Secrets of the Millionaire Mind* (Understanding financial beliefs and habits)
- **Wallace D. Wattles** – *The Science of Getting Rich* (Manifesting wealth through thought and action)

Financial Discipline & Investing

- **Robert Kiyosaki** – *Rich Dad Poor Dad* (Shifting from employee mindset to investor mindset)
- **Benjamin Graham** – *The Intelligent Investor* (Principles of value investing)
- **Vicki Robin & Joe Dominguez** – *Your Money or Your Life* (Financial independence through mindful spending)

Building Multiple Income Streams

- **MJ DeMarco** – *The Millionaire Fastlane* (Entrepreneurship and wealth acceleration)
- **Chris Guillebeau** – *The $100 Startup* (Starting small businesses with minimal investment)
- **Grant Sabatier** – *Financial Freedom* (Creating multiple income streams for financial independence)

Long-Term Wealth & Financial Freedom

- **Thomas J. Stanley & William D. Danko** – *The Millionaire Next Door* (Habits of self-made millionaires)
- **J.L. Collins** – *The Simple Path to Wealth* (Investing for financial independence)
- **Tony Robbins** – *Money: Master the Game* (Strategies for

wealth-building and financial security)

These books provide actionable insights into each step of wealth-building, from mindset shifts to investment strategies. You can explore them further here and here.

https://wealththrifter.com/best-books-for-building-wealth

https://financialmentor.com/free-stuff/best-books

Several television programs in the US and UK have explored wealth-building principles, financial independence, and investing. Here are some notable ones:

UK-Based Shows

- **The Wealth Creation Show** – A UK-based program featuring discussions on financial strategies, investing, and wealth-building.
- **BBC's Money Programme** – A long-running documentary series covering financial trends, business strategies, and economic shifts.
- **Channel 4's** *How the Other Half Live* – Examines wealth disparity and financial habits of the wealthy versus ordinary workers.

US-Based Shows

- **CNBC's** *Mad Money* **with Jim Cramer** – Focuses on stock market investing and financial strategies.
- **PBS's** *The Suze Orman Show* – Offers personal finance advice, budgeting tips, and wealth-building strategies.
- **ABC's** *Shark Tank* – Entrepreneurs pitch business ideas to wealthy investors, showcasing principles of investment and financial growth.
- **CNBC's** *The Profit* – Explores business turnaround

strategies and financial decision-making.

- **ET Money Show** – Covers principles of wealth creation and financial independence.

Online & Video Resources

- **YouTube's** *10 Principles of Building Wealth* – A video series explaining key wealth-building strategies.
- **The Millionaire Next Door Summary** – A breakdown of financial habits of self-made millionaires.

These programs provide valuable insights into financial independence, investing, and wealth-building strategies.

IMPLEMENTATION

100 wealth manifestations is rather a lot to be repeating daily each session. So let's break the number down into managable numbers and still be effective over a week or so

Reciting all 100 wealth manifestations daily would be overwhelming, so structuring them into a digestible routine will enhance focus and effectiveness. Here's a plan for breaking them down while maintaining impact:

Strategic Breakdown

1. **Thematic Clusters** – Organize the 100 manifestations into 10 categories, each focusing on a key aspect of wealth-building (e.g., abundance mindset, financial discipline, passive income, investing wisdom, gratitude, generosity, etc.).
2. **Daily Rotations** – Select 10 manifestations each day, focusing on one category per day. This allows for deep engagement without feeling repetitive.
3. **Morning & Evening Reflection** – Recite five in the morning to set intentions for the day and five in the evening to reinforce belief and gratitude.
4. **Weekly Reinforcement** – Each week, cycle through all 100 manifestations in a structured way, ensuring balanced exposure to all aspects of wealth-building.

Example Weekly Structure

- **Monday:** Mindset & self-worth (10 affirmations)
- **Tuesday:** Financial discipline & smart spending (10 affirmations)
- **Wednesday:** Passive income & investment confidence (10 affirmations)

- **Thursday:** Wealth attraction & financial opportunities (10 affirmations)
- **Friday:** Gratitude & generosity (10 affirmations)
- **Saturday:** Growth & learning (10 affirmations)
- **Sunday:** Vision-setting & success embodiment (10 affirmations)

If 10 still feels too much, you can focus on **5 core manifestations per day** and cycle through them over 20 days instead of a week.

SUMMARY

This book is designed to help you harness the power of manifestation to create financial abundance and lasting prosperity. Through 100 carefully crafted affirmations, you can shift your mindset, reprogram your subconscious, and align yourself with wealth-attracting opportunities.

Manifestation is not just about wishful thinking—it is a powerful tool that combines intention, belief, and action to shape your reality. By consistently focusing on positive wealth-centered affirmations, you cultivate confidence, recognize opportunities, and make decisions that bring financial success closer to you.

Within these pages, you've discovered how to:

- Use manifestation techniques effectively to strengthen your wealth mindset.
- Identify the best times and methods for affirmations to maximize impact.
- Align your emotions and actions with the financial abundance you seek.
- Transform limiting beliefs into empowering ones that

attract prosperity.

Whether you're new to manifestation or looking to refine your practice, this book provides a structured approach to wealth-building through the power of focused intention. Embrace these affirmations daily, stay consistent, and watch as financial success unfolds in your life.

www.ingramcontent.com/pod-product-compliance
Lightning Source LLC
LaVergne TN
LVHW022007200926
848481LV00007B/2273
* 9 7 8 1 0 6 8 2 1 8 8 6 6 *